Prescription for
Happiness
Over 50

Also by Dr. Dorothy Wagner

PRESCRIPTION FOR LIVING
PRESCRIPTION FOR SUCCESS
PRESCRIPTION FOR CHANGE

Prescription for
Happiness
Over 50

Dr. Dorothy Wagner

Fawcett Columbine • New York

Library of Congress Catalog Card Number: 89-91778

ISBN: 0-449-90474-1

Manufactured in the United States of America

First Ballantine Books Edition: August 1990

10 9 8 7 6 5 4 3 2 1

Prescription for
Happiness
Over 50

True maturity is knowing yourself, and that includes accepting your potentials as well as your limitations.

Don't be limited by chronological age. If you have both mental and physical health you have tremendous possibilities.

Most of the things that happen to us and how they happen depend on our state of mind.

We know physical exercise is important, but research shows we need mental exercise as well.

Never lose your curiosity. It is what keeps your mind agile. If you are through learning, you are through!

Don't believe that many of the degenerative diseases that affect people are a necessary part of the aging process.

- Adopt a positive attitude toward life.
- Expect to live a long time.
- More people die of mental dis-ease than of illness.

Keep in touch with your feelings. If you don't you may find that you are exchanging them for physical symptoms.

Stop giving in to colds, aches, pains and all pseudo illnesses.

Stress plays a role in all illnesses from colds to cancer.

Stress lowers the body's immune system thus opening the door to serious disease.

- Avoid self-abuse in any form.
- Practice "self-nurturing" skills.
- Love and be good to yourself.

Egocentricity often comes with aging. It causes people to be perceived as boring and others may choose to avoid them.

Don't envy the young. Youth is often a time of unhappiness. It is not easy for young people to find their place in the world.

Don't believe the myths about aging. The ability to perform sexually is only lost from disease or inactivity.

- Be open to new ideas.
- Try it <u>before</u> you say don't like it!
- Don't deny yourself by limiting your opportunities.

There are no known "anti-aging" drugs or treatments. However, half of the illness in this country is directly related to our behavior.

Smoking related illnesses comprise the largest proportion of preventable diseases.

Eating right will make you very old! The diet for long life is complex carbohydrates, minimal fat, and less protein.

Drink more water. Water is a nutrient second only to oxygen in importance to the body.

Emotional stress, pollution and
dieting are some factors that
make vitamin supplements necessary.

The principle benefit of vitamin C is that it strengthens the immune system. One can take any amount of ascorbic acid without any danger.

After a certain age, and that varies with each of us, maintenance is the key.

New dental techniques, including cosmetic bonding, can provide almost anyone with a great-looking smile.

Whether you are a male or female, don't hesitate to color your hair if you have a mind to do so.

If you can afford it, consider plastic surgery. It is safe, painless, and <u>uplifting</u>.

- Don't save your good clothes, wear them.
- Don't take your possessions for granted, enjoy them.
- Time is your most precious possession, spend it with the ones you love.

Even happy, mentally healthy people feel down at times. Analyze your feelings: have you had a disappointment lately?

Be aware of the "anniversary" phenomenon. You may become overwhelmed by negative feelings near the date of the loss of a loved one.

Remember, our loved ones who have died continue to live in our hearts.

Don't constantly use the personal pronoun "I".

Nothing is more boring to others than listening to someone verbalize their self-pity.

Don't be overly sensitive to slights.

Do you enjoy being the martyr?
Do you wallow in an atmosphere of self-pity?

Keep your mind open to the feelings and problems of others.

If your children don't call or visit, examine your behavior and attitude when they do.

Remember birthdays of those who are
important to you.

Keep in touch with friends as well as relatives.
Build bridges instead of walls.

If you are lucky enough to have grandchildren,
write them, even if they live nearby.
Kids love to get mail!

Without a doubt, good health is your greatest asset.

"Health is a state of complete physical, mental, and social well-being and not merely the absence of disease and infirmity."

—*World Health Organization*

Continue to be physically active, it discourages disease. The absence of exercise invites disease.

Do stretching exercises daily. You must stay flexible to retain the image of vitality.

Take a brisk 20-minute walk each day. It is one of the healthiest things you can do for yourself.

Prevention is the key to longevity, yet physicians are mainly interested in cure and do not make a great effort to prevent illness.

Consult doctors only if you believe that you may be really ill. Do not see the doctor as God.

Avoid hospitalization if possible. Hospitals can be dangerous places and subject you to totally unnecessary medical tests and treatments.

Healing is a natural, biological process. We all carry the best doctor within us. All we need is proper diet, exercise, and rest.

When it's not genetic, death before 100 is due to environmental causes or self-abuse.

Maintain the ability to laugh at yourself. Remember <u>none</u> of us will get out of this alive!